G is for Genghis Khan

A Historic Alphabet Book
from History Unboxed®

HISTORYUNBOXED·

Published by History Unboxed®, LLC
Amissville, VA
Ebook ISBN: 978-1-956571-23-3
Paperback ISBN: 978-1-956571-22-6

Printed in the United States
10 9 8 7 6 5 4 3 2

A Note for Parents and Educators:

Genghis Khan lived a violent life. Please preview this book to make sure it is appropriate for your children. Some content may be upsetting for young or sensitive children.

On the letters: Each alphabet page features a letter filled with textures from Mongolia, including fabric, furs, and feathers.

A is for Asia
Annexed and acquired

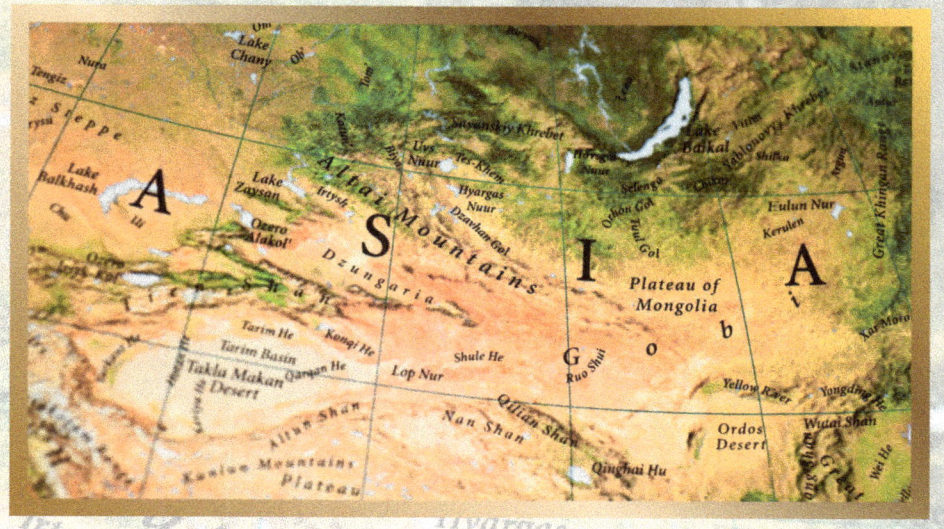

Genghis Khan was a 12th century Mongol leader who conquered huge amounts of territory. It was twice as much as any other single person in history. The final Mongol empire stretched from the Pacific Ocean to Hungary. Three billion people in the world today live in lands once ruled by the Mongols.

B is for Bubonic Plague
Bane of his plans

"Death of Genghis Khan" from *The Travels of Marco Polo*, c. 1410-1412.

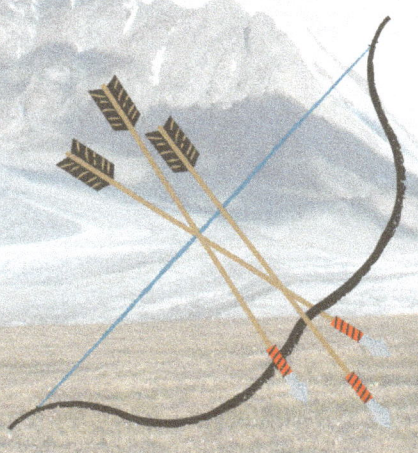

No one knows exactly how Genghis Khan died. Did he tumble off a horse, get stabbed by a princess, fall in battle, or die of an arrow wound? It might have been bubonic plague. Plague had killed thousands of Mongolian soldiers already. The symptoms fit a description of Genghis Khan's death.

C is for Cavalry
Cantering in to conquer

Mongol Cavalry by Rashid al-Din

The Mongol army moved quickly because most of the warriors fought on horseback. They used bow and arrows to attack their enemies. Europeans called them "the devil's horsemen."

D is for Destruction
Deaths, displacements, and dynasties

Mongol Siege by Rashid al-Din

The Mongol empire has a mixed legacy. Genghis Khan destroyed Beijing and many other cities. They made people move to new places if it served the empire. These people introduced their culture and skills to new places. Genghis Khan's descendants conquered more and more territory. His descendants ruled until 1290. Sixteen million people have Genghis Khan as an ancestor.

E is for Emperors
His eminent enemies

Battle between Mongol and Chinese soldiers, Rashid al-Din

When Genghis Khan invaded Jin territory, Emperor Wanyan Yongji wrote to him and said, "Our empire is as vast as the sea. Yours is but a handful of sand. How can we fear you?" Genghis Khan conquered the Jin emperor anyway. He also conquered Emperor Li Anquan in Xia.

F is for Family
Feuding freely

Clockwise from top left: Genghis Khan, Ogedei Khan, Kublai Khan, Temur Khan, Buyantu Khan, Kulug Khan, Jayaatu Khan, Rinchinbal Khan

From getting kicked out of his clan as a child to squabbles with adult siblings, Genghis Khan's family had little peace. He killed his own brother. Then Genghis Khan's children feuded over who would become the next Great Khan.

G is for Genghis Khan
Great or Genocidal?

Unknown Artist, 14th century

The name Genghis Khan comes from Chingis Khan. It means "Universal Ruler." He banned slavery and the selling of women. His empire adopted a writing system. But he also caused famines and destroyed cities. Medieval writers said his armies killed millions of people. Mongolians see him as a hero. Chinese people see him as a ruthless invader.

H is for Hoelun
Honored mother

Mongol Empress Buluqhan Khatun, by
Rashid al-Din

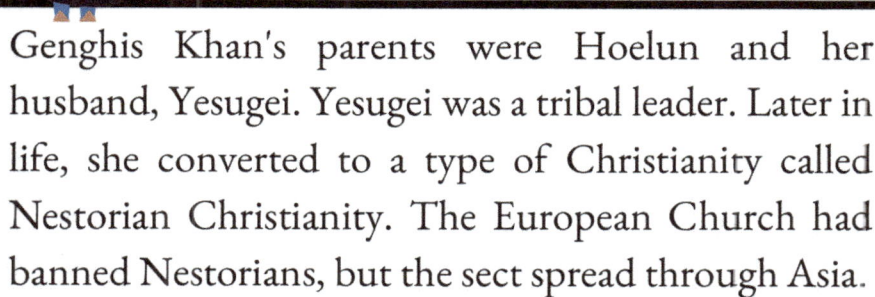

Genghis Khan's parents were Hoelun and her
husband, Yesugei. Yesugei was a tribal leader. Later in
life, she converted to a type of Christianity called
Nestorian Christianity. The European Church had
banned Nestorians, but the sect spread through Asia.

I is for Inalchuq
Instigator of invasion

Genghis Khan wanted to trade with the Khwarezmian Empire. He sent a caravan to the city of Ostra to start the trade talks. But the governor, Inalchuq, thought it was a caravan of spies. He ordered an attack on the caravan. Then Inalchuq's uncle, the Shah Mohammad II, refused to apologize. Genghis Khan ruthlessly invaded the empire with 100,000 soldiers and destroyed city after city.

J is for Jochi
Jealous and Jilted

Jochi was Genghis Khan's oldest son. He was known for being a brave and kind leader. After his father named his brother as heir, Jochi stopped obeying orders. He died of natural causes before his father could act against him.

K is for Kheshig
Keepers of the Khan

The Kheshig were members of an elite imperial guard. Ten thousand loyal warriors guarded the khan every hour of the day. It was an honor and paid well.

L is for Liberator
Larger-than-life in Mongolia

In 2006, modern Mongolians celebrated the 800th anniversary of Genghis Khan's unification of the Mongol tribes. They see it as the beginning of their national identity and celebrate the good parts of his legacy. In 2008, they erected a 130 foot tall statue of him on a horse.

M is for Mongol Empire
Massive and mixed

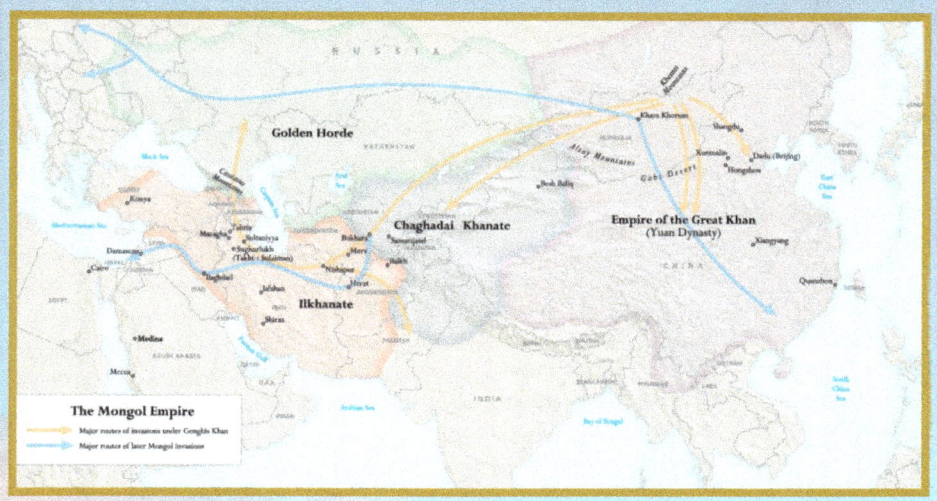

The vast Mongol Empire let cultures connect across thousands of miles. The Mongols helped to organize caravans for traders to travel across the empire. People in the empire spoke dozens of languages and shared knowledge and culture with each other.

N is for Nomadic
No permanent home

Chinggis Khan's Encampment, Rashid al-Din

The Mongols were nomads, people who traveled from place to place instead of having permanent towns and villages. They grazed their animals on the grasslands of Asia and moved with the seasons. The Mongols raised sheep, goats, yaks, camels, and horses. Genghis Khan continued living as a nomad for his entire life.

O is for Ogedei
Official Heir

Coronation of Ogedai, by Rashid al-Din

Genghis Khan's sons Jochi, Chagatai, Tolui, and Ogedei each inherited a khanate (small kingdom), but he made Ogedei the next Great Khan. He built the first Mongol capital city, Khara Khorum. He also liked to have a good time and was known for being easy-going.

P is for Pax Mongolica
Peace through the land

Trade was very important in the Mongol empire. Mongol leaders worked hard to make the roads safe for traders and travelers for a century. This meant Marco Polo could travel from Italy to China and Ibn Battuta could travel from Morocco to China. Chinese travelers visited the courts of England and France.

Q is for Qasar
Quick with a Bow

Mongol Cavalryman, Ming Dynasty

Qasar was one of Genghis Khan's brothers. He led armies for his brother and his descendants had positions of nobility into the 1300s. He had great skill with a bow, and earned the nickname "Qasar the Skillful."

R is for Religiously Tolerant
Rights to rites remained

Erdene zuu monastery near Karakorum Mongolia

Genghis Khan was an animist (believer in nature spirits), but in his empire, he mostly allowed freedom of religion. He gave tax breaks to religious groups like Buddhist monasteries. He took on advisors from different religions.

S is for Shagai

Sheep ankle bones

When Genghis Khan was a boy, he gave a copper filled "knucklebone" to his friend Jamuqa. They played knucklebones together on a frozen river. These knucklebones, called shagai in Mongolian, are actually ankle bones from sheep or horses. Mongolian people still play with shagai today.

T is for Temujin
Tossed out of his tribe

When Genghis Khan was born, his birth name was Temujin. When he was still a little boy, enemies poisoned his father. Temujin's clan kicked out Temujin, his mother, and his six siblings so they would not drain the tribe's resources.

U is for Unification
United Under One Khan

"Genghis Khan s Enthronement," Rashid al-Din, 15th century

Genghis Khan united tribes across the steppes of Asia. Before he united the Mongol people, each tribe had its own leader. The tribes often warred with each other. When a new tribe joined him, he sent members of the tribe to different military units. That way they would be loyal only to him and not the tribal leader.

V is for Vassals
Vowed to serve

Genghis Khan and Chinese Envoys, Rashid al-Din, 1430

Vassals are those who make promises to serve a leader. In the Mongol empire, there were whole vassal states. Mongol vassal states stretched from Russia to Vietnam to Korea.

W is for Wives
Wooed and Wedded

Genghis Khan and Borte, Baswan and Bhim of Gujarat, 1596

Genghis Khan's first wife was Borte. She gave birth to four sons and five daughters. He had six other wives too: Yesugen, Yesui, Khulan, Moge Khantun, Juerbiesu, and Ibaqa Beki.

X is for Xia Conquest
Xanthous River running out of
control

14th century Persian Illustration

Genghis Khan tried to use the Yellow River to flood the capital of Western Xia. His attempt failed, and the river flooded the Mongol camp instead. In the end, Genghis Khan won anyway. (Xanthous means "yellow.")

Y is for Yurts
Yielding to yawns inside

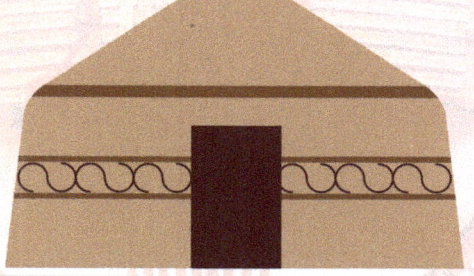

Yurts are large wool-felt tents. They can be transported easily and are very warm. They are so perfect for Mongolian life that Mongolians still use them today. Genghis Khan kept living in one even after he became a successful conqueror. The Mongolian word for yurt is "ger."

Z is for Zhongdu
Zealously defended

Siege of Beijing, Rashid al-Din

Zhongdu was the old name for the city of Beijing. Genghis Khan attacked the city in 1214. Chinese defenders threw everything they had at the Mongols: oil, melted metal, poison, and even poop. In the end, the Mongols won by keeping the people locked in the city until they ran out of food.

Author's Notes

In the study of history, a few persistent ideas keep popping up. One is that history is all about battles and dates. Another is the victors write the history. These ideas get a little complicated when you look closely at one of history's greatest heroes/villains: Genghis Khan.

Genghis Khan was born as Temujin in 1162 (or 1167) to the chief of a Mongol tribe called the Kiyad. The Mongol tribes all operated independently, sometimes forming temporary alliances cemented by political marriages. At nine, Temujin's father took him to the Khonigrad tribe to live with the family of his future wife, Borte. The two children were to marry when Temujin turned twelve. However, on the way home, Temujin's father was killed by Tatars, enemies of the Mongols. Temujin left his place with the Khonigrad in order to assume his father's position as chief, but the tribe kicked Temujin and his family out, leaving them to fend for themselves.

The next few years were a challenging time for Temujin and his family as they fought for survival on the inhospitable Asian steppes. Another tribe kidnapped Temujin and he eventually escaped, a feat that would contribute to his reputation later in life. His enemies had imprisoned him in a yoke, called a cangue. One night, he used the cangue as a weapon against his enemies, swinging it around and leaping into a nearby river. Several members of the enemy tribe helped him escape, later to become some of his most trusted commanders.

Eventually, when he was sixteen, Temujin finally married Borte and cemented the original political alliance his father had hoped for. Yet all was not smooth for the newlyweds. Shortly after the wedding, another Mongol confederation kidnapped Borte. As you can tell from these events, kidnapping was a common political strategy for the Mongol tribes. Temujin rescued Borte, and nine months later, she gave birth to his first son. She went on to bear him three more sons. He also had at least six daughters by other women, although the exact number is unknown. DNA evidence shows that around 8% of men living in the former Mongol empire may be direct descendants of Temujin and his sons. It's a pretty impressive genetic legacy!

While Temujin had a rough start in life, he is most famous for his conquests. By the time of his death, he had united the Mongol tribes into a single empire twice the size of the Roman Empire. It covered over 5 million square miles then and eventually grew to over 9 million square miles over a period of about a century. Given the size of the empire and some of his military tactics it is not surprising that now, nearly a thousand years after his death, opinions on his character and legacy remain mixed. He assumed the title Genghis Khan in 1206, when he accomplished the unification of the Mongol tribes. The name meant "ruler of all." Today, in Turkey, where he is regarded as a military hero, his title is a popular name for boys. He solidified the Silk Road as a trade route by unifying the lands it traversed.

This allowed an increase in both trade and communication from Europe, through the Middle East, and into the heart of Asia. It also became possible for European explorers like Marco Polo to visit Asia and bring back discoveries of the wealth of knowledge available in the Far East. Never had the world seen such a vast cultural exchange. Genghis Khan also introduced gold and silver coins within his empire, as well as some of the world's first paper money. Unlike some of his former rivals, Genghis Khan believed in a system of meritocracy, or ability, rather than hereditary nobility. Because he united the Mongolian tribes, he remains a hero in Mongolia to this day. His empire had an efficient bureaucracy, led by loyal Mongols and run by local administrators. He also promoted religious tolerance within the empire, with two exceptions. And with these two exceptions, we find where Genghis Khan made the most enemies.

Those living in Muslim countries today see him as a vicious warlord. Genghis Khan loathed the religious dietary observances of both Muslims and Jews, and made it illegal for them to follow their religious beliefs regarding the butchering and eating of meat. His invasions of the Iranian plateau were so brutal that one scholar estimates that up to three quarters of the Iranian plateau population died in the conquest, and that the population numbers did not fully recover to pre-Mongol levels until the 20th century. The Mongols under Genghis Khan also destroyed many Eastern European cities. While Genghis Khan was the undisputed victor over millions of square miles, both the image of him as a hero and that of a villain survive today.

About History Unboxed®

History Unboxed® is on a mission to help learners of all ages connect to the people of the past with all five senses through art, recipes, stories, games, and music. Our multi-sensory curriculum and engaging books will help you love every minute of history.

History Unboxed® is an educational company founded in 2014 to bring history to life. Our founder, Elizabeth Hauris, is a second-generation home educator with a background in living history. Her passion for storytelling and hands-on materials led her to create kits to spark curiosity in a new generation. Creative Director Stephanie Hanson, is a former public school educator with experience teaching and raising neurodivergent children.

Let us help you go beyond dates and battles for an engaging, approachable, relatable journey into a story that belongs to all of us -- the history of peoples all over the world.

Learn more about life in
the Mongol Empire
with
Mongols Unboxed
www.historyunboxed.com

Other Books Published
by History Unboxed®

Ancient History: A Secular Exploration of the World by Stephanie Hanson and Elizabeth Hauris

Ancient Eats: An Edible Exploration of the World by Stephanie Hanson

Boards & Bones: A Playful Exploration of the World by Stephanie Hanson and Renee Corbino

A is for Alexander: A Historic Alphabet Book by History Unboxed®

C is for Charlemagne: A Historic Alphabet Book by History Unboxed®

Mysteries of the Rubber People: The Olmecs by Stephanie Hanson

Mysteries of the Shark Hunters: The Jomon by Elizabeth Hauris

The Wizard and the Future King by Elizabeth Hauris and Stephanie Hanson

www.ingramcontent.com/pod-product-compliance
Lightning Source LLC
Chambersburg PA
CBHW051647120626
46551CB00015B/2253